ISBN 978-1-934655-26-0

06-030 • COPYRIGHT © 2006 **World Evangelism Press®**
P.O. Box 262550 • Baton Rouge, Louisiana 70826-2550
Website: www.jsm.org • Email: info@jsm.org
225-768-7000

TABLE OF CONTENTS

CHAPTER   **PAGE**

The Law Of The Spirit

The Cross Of Christ Series

Introduction

THE CROSS OF CHRIST, THE LAW OF THE SPIRIT

INTRODUCTION

There are seven great Laws outlined in the New Testament, all devised and created by God. They are:
1. THE LAW OF GOD (Rom. 7:22);
2. THE LAW OF SIN AND DEATH (Rom. 7:23);
3. THE LAW OF THE MIND (Rom. 7:23);
4. THE LAW OF THE SPIRIT OF LIFE IN CHRIST JESUS (Rom. 8:2);
5. THE LAW OF FAITH (Rom. 3:27);
6. THE LAW OF CHRIST (Gal. 6:2); and,
7. THE LAW OF LIBERTY (James 1:25).

Each one of these seven laws is extremely significant. In this Volume we will, therefore, address all seven, because it is imperative that the Believer understand what each Law means.

LAWS DEVISED BY GOD

Anything devised by the Lord is of extreme significance. It all has to do with our life and living. We should understand what these Laws mean, how they apply to us, and the knowledge that we live with them each and every day of our lives.

The 119th Psalm is the longest Chapter in the Bible. This Psalm is given over to extolling the virtues, power, and life-giving grace of the Word of God. This shows us how significant and important these Laws are. In this 119th Psalm, ten Words are used to describe the Word of God. They are:
1. LAW;
2. WAY;
3. TESTIMONIES;
4. PRECEPTS;
5. COMMANDMENTS;
6. JUDGMENTS;
7. RIGHTEOUSNESS;
8. STATUTES;
9. WORD; and,
10. PATHS.

There are 176 Verses in this Psalm, presented in 22 stanzas. In 172 Verses (that is, all but four Verses), one of these ten Words, exclaiming and extolling the Word of God, is found.

As are all of the Psalms in the Book of Psalms, this 119th Psalm is a Song. They are Songs devised by the Holy Spirit and given to David and others. The 119th Psalm is the longest Song that ever has been written. It is a Song extolling the virtue and glory of the Bible. When we consider that the Holy Spirit has devoted the longest Chapter in the Bible to the fact that the Bible is the road map of life, this tells us just how important all of this is.

(For an in-depth study of all of the Psalms, including the 119th, we recommend *THE JIMMY SWAGGART*

Understanding that all of these Laws were devised by the Lord sometime in eternity past, we should never forget just how important all of them actually are.

SEVEN LAWS

"Seven" is God's number of perfection, totality, and universality. In other words, nothing is missing, nothing is left out, and nothing is misplaced. Whatever God has done, and is doing, is perfect.

Inasmuch as seven Laws were devised by the Lord, these seven Laws impact the entirety of the Word of God all the way from Genesis 1:1 through Revelation 22:21. In some way, the entirety of the Word of God is included in these seven Laws.

Man's number is *"six,"* meaning imperfect, inconclusive, and always falling short of what it ought to be. Only God can round it out, only God can make it complete, and only God can make it perfect. Due to the Fall, man has no perfection in him. Even redeemed man, within himself, has no perfection. All perfection is in Christ and what He has done for us at the Cross.

Considering that these seven Laws address, in some way, the entirety of the Word of God, we should understand just how important they are to our life and living. It is imperative that we understand what they mean, how they affect us, and how they are to be addressed. Hopefully, this Study Guide on this subject will shed some light on this most important teaching of the Word of God.

LAWS

Since these are *"Laws,"* meaning they are binding, and since they were devised by the Lord of Glory sometime in eternity past, we should understand that what these Laws proclaim will come to pass in totality and without fail, that is, if we enter into that respective Law. These are not things that possibly will happen, or that may happen, but these are directions — bondages or freedoms, whichever the case — that most definitely will take place if that particular Law governs us. This we must understand.

Whether the people admit it or not, the entirety of the world, and for all time, testifies to the veracity of these Laws. In other words, if one operates in the *"Law of Sin and Death,"* then one is going to suffer its bondage. Likewise, if one operates in the *"Law of the Spirit of Life in Christ Jesus,"* then one is going to reap the benefits of that Law.

Regrettably, there has been so little teaching on this all-important subject that most Believers have little or no understanding regarding these Laws. Actually, only one of these Laws is negative. That Law is, *"The Law of Sin and Death."* But yet this Law is so powerful, so all-inclusive, and so destructive that it has killed every single human being who has ever lived, with two exceptions — Enoch and Elijah. This Law has filled this Earth with graves and, in many cases, has made life a Hell on Earth.

There is only one defense against this Law, there is only one Law which is more powerful, and that is *"The Law of the Spirit of Life in Christ Jesus."* But yet, just as most Believers understand precious little about *"The Law of Sin and Death,"* they understand even less about *"The Law of the Spirit of Life in Christ Jesus."* And please understand: Ignorance is *not* bliss in these situations. In fact, ignorance is tantamount to death.

Thank God, six of these Laws are positive and only one is negative. However, there is enough pain, destruction, bondage, and darkness in that one Law that it was necessary for God to become Man, come down to this mortal coil, and then die on a Cross; this alone defeated the *"Law of Sin and Death."*

THE CROSS OF CHRIST

The only defense against this *"Law of Sin and Death"* (Rom. 8:2) is the greater *"Law of the Spirit of Life in Christ Jesus,"* which speaks entirely of the Cross (Rom. 6:1-14; 8:2, 11). And as we've already stated, virtually the entirety of the modern Church is ignorant regarding the *"Law of the Spirit of Life in Christ Jesus."* This means that the modern Church understands almost nothing about the Cross of Christ, for that's what the *"Law of the Spirit of Life in Christ Jesus"* actually means. It points directly to the Cross!

The only thing that stands between mankind and eternal Hell is the Cross of Christ.

Likewise, the only thing that stands between the Believer and false doctrine is the Cross of Christ. And false doctrine most definitely can lead to the loss of one's soul and most assuredly to the loss of all victory. If one removes the Cross, one has removed the fiber and the sinew of Christianity. Such *"Christianity"* then is nothing but an empty philosophy, which means that no one will be saved, no lives will be changed, no bondages will be broken, and no power of darkness will be dispelled. All Salvation and all victory are found in the Cross, and they are found *only* in the Cross.

And yet, in the last several decades the Cross of Christ has been relegated in the modern Church to a place of insignificance, if not totally ignored and assigned no place at all. As a result, the Church is following every wind of doctrine and is wandering like a ship without a rudder, seemingly not knowing where it has been, where it is, or where it is going. This situation is all because the modern Church is ignoring, even repudiating, the very foundation of the Gospel, which is the Cross of Christ (Rom. 6:1-14; 8:1-2, 11; I Cor. 1:17-18, 21, 23; 2:2; Gal., Chpt. 5; 6:14; Eph. 2:13-18; Col. 2:14-15).

The modern Church is in worse spiritual condition presently than it has been at any time since the Reformation. Fewer people are truly being saved and fewer Believers are being baptized with the Holy Spirit than ever before. If the Cross is left out of our preaching and out of our believing and out of our understanding of the Word, then the very *"guts"* of Bible Christianity have been removed.

And yet our Lord Jesus predicted this very age, this very time, the condition of the modern Church. He said, and I quote from *THE EXPOSITOR'S STUDY BIBLE*:

"And unto the Angel (Pastor) *of the Church of the Laodiceans write* (this is the *'Apostate Church'*; we do not know when it began, but we do know it has begun; it is the last Church addressed by Christ, so that means the Rapture will take place very shortly); *These things says the Amen, the faithful and true witness* (by contrast to His Church, which is not faithful and true) *the beginning of the Creation of God* (Jesus is the Creator of all things);

"I know your works, that you are neither cold nor hot (characterizes that which is prevalent at this present time): *I would you were cold or hot* (half measures won't do).

"So then because you are lukewarm, and neither cold nor hot (if a person is lukewarm toward something, it means he hasn't rejected it, but at the same time he has by no means accepted it; in the Mind of God, a tepid response is equal to a negative response), *I will spue you out of My mouth.* (There is no prospective of Repentance here on the part of this Church, or Restoration. In fact, there is Divine rejection.)

"Because you say, I am rich, and increased with goods, and have need of nothing (they equated

the increase in material goods with spiritual Blessings, which they were not); *and knowest not that you are wretched, and miserable, and poor, and blind, and naked* (the tragedy lay in the fact that while this Church gloated over material wealth, she was unconscious of her spiritual poverty; again indicative of the modern Church!):

"I counsel you to buy of Me gold tried in the fire, that you may be rich (what they needed to 'buy' could not be purchased with money, but only with the precious Blood of Christ, a price which already has been paid; but the modern Church is not interested!); *and white raiment, that you may be clothed, and that the shame of your nakedness does not appear* (refers to Righteousness which is exclusively of Christ, and is gained only by Faith in Christ and the Cross; this tells us that the Laodicean Church is extremely self-righteous; not having the Righteousness of Christ, they are 'naked' to the Judgment of God); *and anoint your eyes with eyesalve, that you may see.* (The modern Church is also spiritually blind.)

"As many as I love, I rebuke and chasten (implies a remnant): *be zealous therefore, and repent.* (The modern Church desperately needs to repent for its rebellion against God's Divine Order [Christ and the Cross] and following cunningly devised fables [II Pet. 1:16].)

"Behold, I stand at the door, and knock (presents Christ outside the Church): *if any man hear My voice* (so much religious racket is going on that it is difficult to 'hear His Voice'), *and open the door* (Christ is the True Door, which means the Church has erected another door), *I will come in to him, and will sup with him, and he with Me."* (Having been rejected by the Church, our Lord now appeals to individuals, and He is still doing so presently).

And then He said:

"He who has an ear, let him hear what the Spirit says unto the Churches. (In plain language, the Holy Spirit is saying, *'Come back to Christ and the Cross!')"* (Rev. 3:14-20, 22).

The Laodicean Church is known as the apostate Church. Exactly as we have stated, and exactly as our Lord pointed out, it characterizes this modern day.

It would be bad enough if the modern Church was in the process of apostatizing; however, I'm afraid it already has apostatized. This is proclaimed by the fact that Christ is standing outside the Church knocking on the door, trying to get in. It's a chilling indictment!

When the Cross is ignored, even repudiated, as it is presently, the situation is dire indeed! That's the reason it is so imperative that the Preacher of the Gospel *"preach the Cross"* (I Cor. 1:17-18, 21, 23; 2:2).

Chapter 1

The Law Of God

CHAPTER ONE

THE LAW OF GOD

Paul said, *"For I delight in the Law of God* (refers to the moral Law of God ensconced in the Ten Commandments)*, after the inward man* (refers to the spirit and soul of man which have now been regenerated)*"* (Rom. 7:22).

The *"Law of God"* of which Paul speaks is the *"Law of Moses,"* or rather the Law that was given to Moses approximately 1500 years before Christ. It is given in the last twenty Chapters of Exodus and the entire Book of Leviticus. One might say it is broken up into three parts:

1. Moral;
2. Ceremonial; and,
3. Civil.

The moral part basically is ensconced in the Ten Commandments, which are given to us in the Twentieth Chapter of Exodus.

This is the Law that is mentioned over and over again by the Apostle Paul in all of his Epistles. The question must, therefore, be asked:

"Considering that the Apostle Paul's Epistles were written primarily to Gentiles, who had little or no knowledge of the Law of Moses, why did he address the Law so much?"

There was a reason that the Holy Spirit directed so much attention to the Law of Moses. When the Bible writers penned these Books and Epistles, they were not merely giving their own thoughts about the subject, whatever the subject may have been, but they were inspired by the Holy Spirit to write on each particular subject matter. Inspiration can be explained to such a degree that the Holy Spirit, in every instance, searched through the vocabulary of each Bible writer, seeking the exact word that He desired. In other words, these men who wrote the Books and Epistles of the Bible, even beginning with Moses, did not give their own glosses and shadings, but rather wrote exactly what the Holy Spirit wanted to be written, down to the very word in each sentence.

That's the reason it is imperative that Believers have a word-for-word translation of the Bible, such as the King James Version. A thought-for-thought translation is actually no Bible at all! The many paraphrases that glut today's market are not Bibles in the true sense of the word, but rather religious meanderings.

Jesus said:

"Man shall not live by bread alone, but by every Word that proceeds out of the Mouth of God" (Mat. 4:4).

Whatever the Apostle Paul wrote, he was inspired by the Holy Spirit to do so. He wrote exactly what the Holy Spirit wanted and desired. To be sure, the Holy Spirit gave us exactly what we need.

So, as we go along, we will come to the place where we will see why the Holy Spirit directed so much attention through the Apostle Paul to the Law of Moses. If the modern Reader thinks that this instruction does not apply to him, he is altogether missing the point and is setting himself up for a Fall.

Remember, Jesus said, *". . . every Word that proceeds out of the Mouth of God."*

WHAT IS THE LAW OF GOD?

The Law of Moses (Law of God) was, and is, God's Standard of Righteousness. It is His moral Law, which is demanded of all men, and for all time.

In fact, every Civil Law in the world which provides even a modicum of Righteousness in its instruction is, in some way, derived from the Ten Commandments. Presently, there is no Civil Law in the U.S. which says, *"You shall not commit adultery"* (Ex. 20:14), but this one Commandment covers every aspect of moral law regarding sexual immorality.

For instance, whatever type of laws are on the books of any City or State forbidding indecent exposure, child molestation, etc., they all stem from this one Commandment in the Twentieth Chapter of the Book of Exodus, whether or not the legislators who wrote and passed the laws knew it.

In some way, all the Commandments form a base or foundation on which all sensible and reasonable law in the world is built. As stated, the legislators may or may not know and understand that, but it is the truth nonetheless.

When any nation of the world abrogates these Commandments — by permitting abortion on demand, for example — then the downward slide commences, even as is currently occurring here in the U.S.

God formulated these Laws for mankind. He did not do it for Angels, but altogether for humanity. To be sure, these Laws were instituted for purpose and reason, that is, for the good of humanity. Of that one can be certain!

At the same time, we must understand that Righteousness cannot be legislated. But there must be a Standard or moral code, and man cannot set that moral code; only God can do so.

THE LAW AND THE PENALTY

If anything constitutes a *"Law,"* it must have a penalty. To be sure, the Law of God most definitely has penalties.

If the Law is broken, the penalty is death. By death, we refer to separation from God. Certain parts of the Law of God demanded the loss of life, but this was carried out very rarely (Ex. 21:12-17).

These capital crimes were: *"murder," "parental dishonor,"* and *"kidnapping."* Breaking the Sabbath also was punishable by death (Ex. 31:15), and there also were other capital crimes.

Some may think it's rather severe for the death penalty to attach to breaking the Sabbath and certain other violations; however, there was a reason for this, which I will not now take the time to explain.

In a sense, the Law of God only applied to Israel. In the strict sense of the word, that is not exactly correct, but yet the Gentile world had absolutely no way to be saved unless one became a proselyte Jew. In other words, the Gentiles were not in the Covenant; and, to be saved, one had to be in the Covenant. This Covenant covered the entirety of Israel; but, at the same time, there was also only a small Remnant in Israel who truly served the Lord and who truly were saved. That's the way it always was. In fact, that's the way it is in the modern Church presently (Rom. 9:27; 11:5).

Very few Israelites actually were executed because, for execution to be carried out, there had to be two or more witnesses to the capital crime (Num. 35:30; Deut. 17:6). In modern courts of law, even one reliable eyewitness to a capital crime may be sufficient to result in execution. But under the Mosaic Law, one witness would not suffice. There had to be two or more.

So, under Old Testament Law, not many executions were carried out.

THE SACRIFICIAL SYSTEM

A great part of the Mosaic Law was the Sacrificial System installed by the Lord. It would serve as the means by which forgiveness could be enjoined and fellowship restored regarding the individual who had sinned. Without this system, Israel would have been totally destroyed.

The Sacrificial System, which consisted of five Sacrifices (The Whole Burnt Offering, The Sin Offering, The Trespass Offering, The Meal Offering, and The Peace Offering), were a forepicture of the Sacrifice of Christ, which was yet to come. So the Cross of Christ stands out in the Mosaic Law as the greatest part of that Law, because it is the part that gave man hope.

As stated, without the Sacrificial System, Israel would have been destroyed. It is the same presently. The Cross of Christ is the only thing that stands between mankind and eternal Hell.

THE DEMANDS OF GOD

God demanded that this Law be kept, as well He should! If a Law is to be valid, the penalty for breaking the Law must be enforced.

And yet, the Lord had a problem in this area. Fallen man is totally incapable of keeping the Law. This even included God's chosen people, the Israelites. When one looks at the Ten Commandments which form the foundation of the moral law, they may seem simple enough, but fallen man simply is unable to keep these Commandments. No matter how hard he tries, he might keep some of them, but there is no way he can keep all of them.

And the Holy Spirit through James pointedly says, *"For whosoever shall keep the whole Law, and yet offend in one point, he is guilty of all"* (James 2:10).

Now it might seem cruel for God to give a Law and demand that man keep that Law, when He knew all the time that it would be impossible for man to succeed in this. The Law of God carried a severe penalty (as does all Law) but it provided no power to help fallen man to obey its injunctions. The Law was like a mirror; it shows man what he is, but gives him no power to change what he is.

Furthermore, if God had given man the ability and power to keep the Law, this would not have solved the problem at all. It only would have exacerbated the problem, that is, the situation only would have been made worse.

Man's problem is pride. To break that pride, God had to give man His Standards — fair, righteous, and equitable Standards — in order that man would see he was incapable of keeping the Law. Then man was to throw himself on the Mercy of God through the Sacrificial System, trusting in the One Who was to come and Who was portrayed by the Sacrificial System. Man had to admit his incapability and lean totally on the Lord for hope and forgiveness.

Unfortunately, only a few Israelites did this which the Lord had planned. Most went about attempting to establish their own Righteousness, which ultimately destroyed the entire nation (Rom. 10:1-3).

So the problem was not that God was remiss in not giving Israel the strength and ability to keep the Law, but rather that Israel rejected His Plan for Redemption, which pointed out their true problem and the remedy.

That remedy is, and always has been, *"Jesus Christ and Him Crucified,"* which was symbolized by the Sacrificial System of the Old Testament (Gen., Chpt. 4).

This is the major problem: Man always has resisted God's Word. Man attempts to institute his own word, which always leads to destruction.

Solomon said, *"There is a way which seems right unto a man, but the end thereof are the ways of death"* (Prov. 14:12).

THE CURSE OF THE BROKEN LAW

Every single unsaved person in the world still comes under the penalty of the Law of God. If they do not make the Lord Jesus Christ the Saviour of their souls, they one day will stand before God at the Great White Throne Judgment and answer to this Law. It doesn't make any difference that most of the world doesn't even believe in God or His Law. All who reject Christ will answer to that Law.

The Law of God defines what sin is and puts it in ten different categories, which refer to the Ten Words, that is, The Ten Commandments (Ex., Chpt. 20).

Referring to Christ and His Death on the Cross, Paul said, *"Christ has redeemed us from the curse of the Law, being made a curse for us: for it is written, Cursed is every one who hangs on a tree"* (Gal. 3:13). The Death of Christ on the Cross satisfied the curse of the broken Law, at least for those who will accept Christ. For those who reject Christ, the curse remains and the penalty is death (Rom. 6:23).

Paul also said, *"For Christ is the end of the Law for Righteousness* (Christ fulfilled the totality of the Law) *to every one who believes.* (Faith in Christ guarantees the Righteousness which the Law had, but could not give)*"* (Rom. 10:4).

The meaning of this Verse is this: Christ satisfied the Law in every respect.

Through His entire Life, He perfectly kept the Law in every respect. He never failed, not even one time, whether in thought, word, or deed. Even though Christ perfectly kept the Law, the problem of the broken Law remained. The broken Law could be satisfied only by Christ going to the Cross and offering up Himself as a Perfect Sacrifice, which He did, which satisfied in totality the righteous demands of the Law.

That's what Paul was talking about when he said, *"Blotting out the handwriting of Ordinances that was against us* (pertains to the Law of Moses, which was God's Standard of Righteousness that man could not reach), *which was contrary to us* (Law is against us, simply because we are unable to keep its precepts, no matter how hard we try), *and took it out of the way* (refers to the penalty of the Law being removed), *nailing it to His Cross* (the Law with its decrees was abolished in Christ's Death, as if crucified with Him)*"* (Col. 2:14).

Whenever the individual accepts Christ as his own personal Saviour, the Law is thereby satisfied, meaning that it no longer is held against the individual and it has no claim. It has all been satisfied in Christ. This is what Paul meant when he said that Christ is the end of the Law.

17

THE CHRISTIAN AND THE LAW

The Law was finished with Christ for those who will trust Christ, but the modern Church still finds itself neck-deep in Law.

How do I know that?

The answer — the only answer — to the Law is the Cross of Christ. Regrettably, the modern Church little preaches the Cross anymore, and a great part of the Church actually repudiates the Cross.

So, if the Cross of Christ is not the sole Object of our Faith, then Law is the only other alternative.

What confuses most Christians is that they know and believe that the Law of Moses is not at all active within their lives, but yet they are entangled with laws made up by themselves, their Church, their Denomination, some Preacher, etc. Even though it's not the Law of Moses, it still is Law, and it will bring about the same results — failure.

Most modern Christians, in fact, have made *"Laws"* out of things which, in their own right, are perfectly legitimate. It is even possible to turn prayer into a law.

And how can one do that?

If the Believer thinks that he can pray so much each day to guarantee victory over sin, to his dismay he will find that such is not the case. The only answer for sin is the Cross of Jesus Christ. But the modern Church little believes what we've just stated, as simple as the statement is. Consequently, it reverts to Law, while all the while it trumpets Grace.

If the Believer doesn't understand the Cross regarding Sanctification (and almost none do!), which is the teaching of the Sixth Chapter of the Book of Romans, such a person is going to revert to Law, because there is no other place to be. It is either *"Law"* or *"Grace."* We must understand that Grace functions strictly within the parameters of the Finished Work of Christ, that is, *"the Cross."*

The entire Seventh Chapter of Romans is a portrayal of Paul's personal experience at trying to live for God by means of Law. The end result of that is, and I quote from *THE EXPOSITOR'S STUDY BIBLE*:

"For that which I do (the failure) *I allow not* (should have been translated, *'I understand not'*; these are not the words of an unsaved man, as some claim, but rather a Believer who is trying and failing): *for what I would, that do I* not (refers to the obedience he wants to render to Christ, but rather fails. Why? As Paul explained, the Believer is married to Christ, but is being unfaithful to Christ by spiritually cohabiting with the Law, which frustrates the Grace of God; that means the Holy Spirit will not help such a person, which guarantees failure [Gal. 2:21])*; but what I hate, that do I* (refers to sin in his life, which he doesn't want to do, and in fact hates, but

finds himself unable to stop; unfortunately, due to the fact of not under-standing the Cross as it refers to Sanctification, this is the plight of most modern Christians)" (Rom. 7:15).

In Paul's defense, although the Seventh Chapter of Romans portrays the Apostle's own personal experience, it pertains to the time of his Christian experience before the Lord Jesus Christ gave him the Revelation of the Cross (Gal. 1:11-12). Again in his defense, no one else at that time understood the Message of the Cross.

The meaning of the New Covenant is the Cross of Christ. One also might say the Cross of Christ is the meaning of the New Covenant. The Lord explained to Paul what the New Covenant meant, which was all wrapped up in the Cross (I Cor. 1:17-18, 21, 23; 2:2).

SPIRITUAL ADULTERY

The Believer is married to Christ (Rom. 7:4), and should look strictly to Christ for all things, which pertains to what He did for us at the Cross. When the Believer instead looks to other things, such constitutes spiritual adultery. In other words, such a Believer is being unfaithful to Christ.

(The Reader should refer to our Study Guide, *THE CROSS OF CHRIST, Spiritual Adultery*.)

This means the Holy Spirit will not help such a person. This translates into spiritual failure of one type or another. Without the Holy Spirit, the Believer is not going to be able to live for God, at least not as he ought to. Tragically, even though the Holy Spirit does not leave the heart and life of the failing Believer, still, He is greatly hindered in His help to us because He most definitely cannot condone our status or state of spiritual adultery, which is gross sin.

And without the help of the Holy Spirit, the Believer is not going to be able to live the life he ought to live — not at all! (Rom. 8:1-2, 11).

Because it is so very, very important, please allow me to say it again:

The Believer either is functioning in the realm of Grace or Law. There is no other place for him to be. Tragically, due to the fact that the modern Church understands not at all the Cross as it regards Sanctification, virtually the entirety of the modern Church is functioning in the realm of *"Law,"* whether or not they realize it. As a result, they will function exactly as did Paul; they will try to do that which is right and fail, and they will try to not do that which is wrong, and do it anyway (Rom. 7:15).

Moreover, those who would claim that the Seventh Chapter of Romans refers to Paul's experience before his conversion are only fooling themselves.

First of all, what good would that do?

No, even a cursory examination of the Seventh Chapter of Romans proclaims the fact that we are dealing here with a man who is saved, baptized with the Holy Spirit, and trying his best to live for God, but who is failing, because he's doing it in all the wrong ways.

And, if it happened to Paul, it will happen to any and all who follow in the train of Law.

LAW-KEEPER

When the believing sinner accepts Christ, he is automatically transferred from the position of lawbreaker and all of the resultant penalties to the position of law-keeper, all because of Christ and what Christ did for us at the Cross.

If our faith is placed in Christ and what Christ did for us at the Cross, and if our faith remains in Christ and what Christ did for us at the Cross, Law will be no problem whatsoever, which means the sin nature will be no problem, simply because we are functioning by faith placed in the correct object, which is Christ and Him Crucified. In a nutshell, that is God's Prescribed Order of Victory.

In this capacity, the Believer doesn't even have to think about the Law, or sin for that matter. The one who is totally trusting in Christ and what Christ did at the Cross doesn't worry about keeping the Commandments, because they already are kept. It is all done in Christ, with the Believer resting secure in that Finished Work.

If the Believer resorts to Law in any fashion, he will find himself failing, actually dreading to face each day. He will scheme and plan trying to find ways not to fail the Lord, but will always conclude by failing. Such a position does not exactly describe *"more abundant life,"* which is promised to us by Christ (Jn. 10:10). Such a person may be saved, but they are *"miserably saved"*!

That is not God's Way. His Way is Jesus Christ as the Source and the Cross as the Means. That's why Jesus came to this world. He came here to satisfy the demands of the broken Law, which would also satisfy the demands of a thrice-Holy God. He would do such by going to the Cross and there offering up Himself as a Sacrifice, which He did, and which provided a Finished Work.

Let us say it again:

"But when the fullness of the time was come (which completed the time designated by God that should elapse before the Son of God would come), *God sent forth His Son* (it was God Who acted; the Law required man to act; this requirement demonstrated man's impotency; the Son of God requires nothing from man other than his confidence), *made of a*

woman (pertains to the Incarnation, God becoming Man), *made under the Law* (refers to the Mosaic Law; Jesus was subject to the Jewish legal economy, which He had to be, that is, if He was to redeem fallen humanity; in other words, He had to keep the Law perfectly, which no human being had ever done, but He did),

"To redeem them who were under the Law (in effect, all of humanity is under the Law of God, which man, due to his fallen condition, could not keep; but Jesus came and redeemed us by keeping the Law perfectly, and, above all, satisfying its penalty on the Cross, which was death), *that we might receive the adoption of sons* (that we could become the sons of God by adoption, which is carried out by faith in Christ and what He did at the Cross)" (Gal. 4:4-5).

The answer to Law — the only answer to Law — is *"Jesus Christ and Him Crucified"* (I Cor. 1:23). Consequently, the Cross of Christ must ever be the Object of the Believer's Faith.

WHY IS THE CROSS OF CHRIST SUCH AN OFFENSE?

The teaching we have given in this Volume is very simple. Even a child can understand it. And yet, it is rejected by most Christians, which guarantees spiritual failure, and for many will result in the loss of their soul. There could be nothing worse than that.

Why is the Cross of Christ such an offense to many? Even most Believers?

First of all, most Believers would deny that the Cross is an offense to them. But yet, they do not accept the Cross as the answer to man's dilemma, but rather other things.

Paul said the following:

"And I, Brethren, if I yet preach circumcision, why do I yet suffer persecution? (Any message other than the Cross draws little opposition.) *Then is the offense of the Cross ceased.* (The Cross offends the world and most of the Church. So, if the Preacher ceases to preach the Cross as the only way of Salvation and Victory, then opposition and persecution will cease. But so will Salvation!)" (Gal. 5:11).

The Cross of Christ is an offense for many reasons. First of all, the Cross denies all of man's efforts, abilities, strengths, plus anything and everything that he can do to save himself or to bring about victory within his life. Prideful man doesn't enjoy coming face-to-face with his helplessness; and, to be sure, the Cross of Christ makes man face up to that problem.

Man, even believing man, loves to think that he can solve his own problems, work out his own situation, and bring about the desired results by his own efforts. That's the reason that man, even the Church, has opted for humanistic psychology. He refuses to give up the idea that his condition can only be addressed by the Holy Spirit, Who functions entirely within the parameters of the Finished Work of Christ.

When modern Christians speak of placing their faith in Christ and the Cross, they are speaking only of Salvation. Regrettably, even that is getting lost in the shuffle. When one speaks of the Cross and Sanctification, most Christians look at you with a blank stare. They simply don't know what you are talking about. The pulpits are silent on the subject because the Preacher little knows or understands the meaning of the Sixth Chapter of Romans.

Most think that Romans 6:3-5 pertains to Water Baptism. It doesn't!

It pertains to the Death of our Saviour on the Cross, His Burial, and Resurrection. More particularly, it pertains to us dying with Him, being buried with Him, and raised with Him in newness of life. This is the very epitome and core of the Christian experience. On the subject of properly living for God, Paul also said:

"*I am crucified with Christ* (as the foundation of all Victory; Paul, here, takes us back to Romans 6:3-5)*: nevertheless I live* (have new life)*; yet not I* (not by my own strength and ability)*, but Christ lives in me* (by virtue of me dying with Him on the Cross, and being raised with Him in newness of life)*: and the life which I now live in the flesh* (my daily walk before God) *I live by the Faith of the Son of God* (the Cross is ever the Object of my Faith), *Who loved me, and gave Himself for me* (which is the only way that I could be saved)*"* (Gal. 2:20).

Then Paul adds to that a very informative statement by saying further:

"*I do not frustrate the Grace of God* (if we make anything other than the Cross of Christ the Object of our Faith, we frustrate the Grace of God, which means we stop its action, and the Holy Spirit will no longer help us)*: for if Righteousness come by the Law* (any type of Law), *then Christ is dead in vain.* (If I can successfully live for the Lord by any means other than Faith in Christ and the Cross, then the Death of Christ was a waste)*"* (Gal. 2:21).

FRUSTRATING THE GRACE OF GOD

And that's exactly what most modern Believers are doing. They are frustrating the Grace of God. When we place our faith in anything other than Christ and the Cross, this automatically stops the flow of Grace and all the action of the Holy Spirit on our behalf. This is so ironclad that Paul said that if we can gain Righteousness by any means other than through Christ and the Cross, "*then Christ is dead in vain,*" meaning He died needlessly.

All of this emphatically states that it's not possible for a Believer to walk in victory by adhering to Law in any fashion. All he tends to do is to frustrate the Grace of God, which then stops all victorious living. The simple truth is, most modern Christians simply don't know how to live for God. Regrettably, the Churches are filled with Preachers telling people in all the wrong ways how to live for the Lord. If it's not the Cross of Christ, then it's wrong!

Let me say it again:

No matter how good it may look on the surface, no matter how good it might sound, if it's not the Cross of Christ, then, whatever it is, it's a waste of time. Regrettably, that characterizes virtually the entirety of that which is offered by most Preachers.

The terrible truth is, most Preachers do not know how to live for God themselves.

So how can they help others?

The truth is, they can't!

This Chapter may be summed up with these words: Christ is the Source of all things from God, while the Cross is the Means.

LAW AND LAWS

Even though we have already alluded to the following, still, because of the significance of the subject, I think it would be proper to go into a little more detail.

When the *"Law of Moses,"* is mentioned, most Christians dismiss it out of hand, thinking that it does not apply to us presently. In a sense that is true; however, why do you think that the Apostle Paul dealt with the Law of Moses so much? He was mostly writing to Gentiles in his Epistles, and as a matter of fact, they knew next to nothing about the Law of Moses. We know that the Holy Spirit moved upon him to write exactly what he did, and for purpose.

He dealt with it so extensively simply because it was a problem then, and to be sure, it is a problem now.

There is something in the human being, which no doubt is a product of the Fall, which thinks that we have the capacity to do what we need to do as it regards living for God. In other words, we think we can keep the Law. And yet, concerning this, Paul said, *"And if Christ be in you* (He is in you through the Power and Person of the Spirit [Gal. 2:20]), *the body is dead because of sin* (means that the physical body has been rendered helpless because of the Fall; consequently, the Believer trying to overcome by will-power presents a fruitless task)*; but the Spirit is life because of Righteousness* (only the Holy Spirit can make us what we ought to be, which means we cannot do it ourselves; once again, He performs all that He does within the confines of the Finished Work of Christ)" (Rom. 8:10).

Let us say it again: due to the Fall, the physical body is rendered helpless, at least as it concerns doing what we need to do as a Believer to successfully live for the Lord. Now, most Christians do not understand this. They think that because they are saved and baptized with the Holy Spirit, that they now have the power to do whatever it is that needs to be done. In fact, that is true, but not in the way they think.

Again Paul says, *"But if the Spirit* (Holy Spirit) *of Him* (from God) *Who raised up Jesus from the dead dwell in you* (and He definitely does)*, He Who raised up Christ from the dead shall also quicken your mortal bodies* (give us power in our mortal bodies that we might live a victorious life) *by His Spirit Who dwells in you* (we have the same power in us, through the Spirit, that raised Christ from the dead, and is available to us only on the premise of the Cross and our Faith in that Sacrifice)" (Rom. 8:11).

So, in this Eleventh Verse, the Apostle Paul tells us that these mortal bodies can be quickened, which means to be made alive, and done so by the Holy Spirit; however, the working of the Holy Spirit within our physical bodies is not an automatic thing. While the Lord doesn't require much of us, He does require that our Faith be placed exclusively in Christ and the Cross in order for the Holy Spirit to work within our lives (Rom. 8:1-2). And that way the Law is kept, and we speak of the moral law, and done so gloriously, but only in the manner given.

LAWS OF OUR OWN DEVISING

While the Law of Moses, as stated, is not too very much the problem in the modern Church, still, the propensity to make and keep laws as a Child of God is ever with is. What do I mean by that?

While it's not so much the Law of Moses that Believers attempt to live by, it most definitely is *"laws"* which are made up and devised by the Church, or Denomination, or Preachers, or we devise them ourselves. We don't think of them as laws, but they are, and how do I know that?

Anything that's not simply faith in Christ and the Cross, in which we place our faith, is a law. In fact, we Christians are very bad about taking things which are perfectly legitimate and right, actually greatly beneficial, and turning them into laws. Let me give you an example!

I was watching a Preacher over Television recently. He was telling the people that if they will take the Lord's Supper everyday, or some such length of time, that they will walk in victory, be successful, etc. While the Lord's Supper is definitely a proper ordinance and, in fact, very sacred, still, one can take the Lord's Supper ten thousand times; and it will afford no victory over sin, or victory in any capacity for that matter. Our dear brother had turned this beautiful ordinance into a *"law,"* and all who listen to him and subscribe to what he is saying, are doing the same thing.

One can even turn prayer into a law. While prayer is a discipline that every good Christian should engage in constantly, as should be obvious; however, if one thinks that one can pray so much each day, and thereby gain victory over sin, it will not happen. The individual has just turned this most wonderful attribute into a *"law,"* which the Lord can never bless.

While the person engaging in such, might be blessed in other ways, he or she will never find victory within their lives by this method.

In fact, almost all of the modern Church is attempting to live for God in one way or the other, by means of law. They don't think of it as law, and would no doubt argue that it's not law; however, it most definitely is!

HOW DO WE RECOGNIZE LAW?

To cut straight through to the bottom line, whatever it is in which one has placed one's faith, if it's not the Cross of Christ and the Cross of Christ exclusively, then it is *"law."* Pure and simple it is law! And that's man's big problem.

Man, and especially religious man, loves to make laws, and to project those laws, even though they may be called something else, as the way to victory, etc. Man has yet to learn that due to the Fall, he cannot keep laws, irrespective as to how simple they might be. In fact, this problem is so acute that God had to become Man, come down here and die on a Cross in order that man might be saved. That's the reason that Paul said, and I quote from *THE EXPOSITOR'S STUDY BIBLE*: *"I do not frustrate the Grace of God* (if we make anything other than the Cross of Christ the object of our faith, we frustrate the Grace of God, which means we stop its action, and the Holy Spirit will no longer help us)*: for if righteousness come by the Law* (any type of Law), *then Christ is dead in vain.* (If I can successfully live for the Lord by any means other than Faith in Christ and the Cross, then the Death of Christ was a waste)*"* (Gal. 2:21).

Chapter 2

The Law Of Sin And Death

CHAPTER TWO

THE LAW OF SIN AND DEATH

Paul said, *"For the Law* (that which we are about to give is a Law of God, devised by the Godhead in eternity past [I Pet. 1:18-20]; this Law, in fact, is *'God's Prescribed Order of Victory'*) *of the Spirit* (Holy Spirit, that is, *'the Way the Spirit works'*) *of Life* (all life comes from Christ, but through the Holy Spirit [Jn. 16:13-14]) *in Christ Jesus* (any time Paul uses this term or one of its derivatives, he is, without fail, referring to what Christ did at the Cross, which makes this *'life'* possible) *has made me free* (given me total Victory) *from the Law of Sin and Death* (these are the two most powerful Laws in the Universe; the *'Law of the Spirit of Life in Christ Jesus'* alone is stronger than the *'Law of Sin and Death'*; this means that if the Believer attempts to live for God by any manner other than Faith in Christ and the Cross, he is doomed to failure)*"* (Rom. 8:2).

Even though in this one Verse Paul deals with both the *"Law of the Spirit of Life in Christ Jesus"* and the *"Law of Sin and Death,"* we will deal only with the latter at this time.

The *"Law of Sin and Death"* is the second most powerful Law on the face of the Earth, second only to the *"Law of the Spirit of Life in Christ Jesus."*

The *"Law of Sin and Death"* came into being with the Fall of man in the Garden of Eden.

Sin constitutes a disobedience of God's Laws and Commandment — in other words, a transgression of His Word. Death always follows sin, which refers, first of all, to separation from God, which refers to separation from all life. In a sense, it also refers to the death of everything that sinful man touches. It is the cause of all the heartache, war, destruction, pain, sickness, suffering, and man's inhumanity to man, which characterizes the world now and has done so ever since the Fall.

The *"Law of Sin and Death"* is so powerful that the only Law that can overcome it is, the *"Law of the Spirit of Life in Christ Jesus."* That is why it is so foolish for the Church to resort to humanistic psychology. Such holds no answers, never will have any answers, and actually leads one in the opposite direction from the true help that can be received from our Lord.

THE MODERN CHURCH AND SIN

In much of the modern Church growth concepts, the word *"sin"* no longer is used, because it might offend someone. So the problem of sin is addressed as a disease, a mistake, a wrong direction, or any other way that would not offend people.

"Sin" is a Biblical term. Because it is a Biblical term, it does offend many people. Most do not like to admit that their problem is sin. But please read the following very carefully:

The problem the world over is sin, and the only solution is Christ and Him Crucified (I Cor. 1:17-18, 21, 23; 2:2).

Every true Revival that ever has touched the Church always, and without exception, has been accompanied by a consciousness of sin and a fear of the Wrath of God.

God is unalterably opposed to sin in any form. He cannot abide sin, cannot tolerate sin, and He must judge sin wherever it is found.

The Scripture says:

"For the Wrath of God (God's Personal emotion with regard to sin) is revealed from Heaven (this anger originates with God) against all ungodliness and unrighteousness of men (God must unalterably be opposed to sin), who hold the truth in unrighteousness (who refuse to recognize Who God is and What God is)" (Rom. 1:18).

THE DEPTH OF SIN

From the Old Testament Sacrifices we learn the depths of sin.

When the animal was killed (the lamb), the skin was pulled from its body to show that sin is not merely a surface problem. Then the intestines and fat were taken out and burned on the Altar to show that sin goes to the very core of a person's being. As stated, it is not merely a wrong direction or a surface problem, but actually originates with the heart, which is the seat of one's emotions, one's very being. One might say that the "heart," as used in the Bible, refers to the soul and the spirit of man.

Concerning this, Jesus said:

"For out of the heart proceed evil thoughts, murders, adulteries, fornications, thefts, false witness, blasphemies (this proclaims the depravity of the unconverted human heart, which was the condition of the Pharisees, despite their religiosity):

"These are the things which defile a man . . . (Satan is a master at placing the emphasis on the insignificant, instead of the real problem)" (Mat. 15:19-20).

THE ONLY SOLUTION TO THE LAW OF SIN AND DEATH IS THE CROSS OF CHRIST

The entirety of the story of the Bible is "Jesus Christ and Him

Crucified" (I Cor. 1:23).

The principle or Doctrine of the Cross of Christ is the primary doctrine of the entirety of the Plan of Redemption. Sometime in eternity past, God, by the means of foreknowledge, even before the foundation of the world, knew that He would make man and that man would fall.

At that time, whenever it was, the Godhead formulated the Plan of Redemption, which required God to become Man and to die on a Cross, which would pay the price for man's Redemption. Love created man, so love must redeem man.

Concerning this, Peter said:

"Forasmuch as you know that you were not Redeemed with corruptible things, as silver and gold (presents the fact that the most precious commodities [silver and gold] could not redeem fallen man), *from your vain conversation* (vain lifestyle) *received by tradition from your fathers* (speaks of original sin that is passed on from father to child at conception);

"But with the Precious Blood of Christ (presents the payment, which proclaims the poured out Life of Christ on behalf of sinners), *as of a Lamb without blemish and without spot* (speaks of the lambs offered as substitutes in the Old Jewish economy; the Death of Christ was not an execution or assassination, but rather a Sacrifice; the Offering of Himself presented a Perfect Sacrifice, for He was Perfect in every respect [Ex. 12:5]):

"Who verily was foreordained before the foundation of the world (refers to the fact that God, in His Omniscience, knew He would create man, man would fall, and man would be Redeemed by Christ going to the Cross; this was all done before the Universe was created; this means the Cross of Christ is the Foundation Doctrine of all doctrine, referring to the fact that all doctrine must be built upon that Foundation, or else it is specious), *"but was manifest in these last times for you* (refers to the invisible God, Who, in the Person of the Son, was made visible to human eyesight by assuming a human body and human limitations)*"* (I Pet. 1:18-20).

Paul said, *"According as He has chosen us in Him* (does not refer to the person being chosen, but rather the purpose for which the person is chosen) *before the foundation of the world* (the Creator, in laying His Plans for the world, had the purpose of Redeeming Grace in view . . .)*"* (Eph. 1:4).

John the Beloved said, *"And all who dwell upon the Earth shall worship him* (first of all, we are speaking here of worship, not dominion of nations; as well, the word *'all'* doesn't refer to every single human being, but rather people from all nations of the world, however many that number might be), *whose names are not written in the Book of Life* (refers to the fact that Believers will not worship the Antichrist) *of the Lamb slain from the foundation of the world.* (This tells us that the only way one's name can be placed in the Book of Life is by acceptance of Jesus Christ as one's Lord and Saviour, and what He did for us at the Cross. Also, the phrase, *'From the foundation of the world,'* proclaims the fact that the Doctrine of *'Jesus Christ and Him Crucified'* is the Foundation Doctrine of all doctrines. In other words, every doctrine from the Bible must be built on the Foundation of the Cross of Christ; otherwise it is bogus)" (Rev. 13:8).

All of this tells us just how important the Cross of Christ actually is. As previously stated, if one takes out the Cross, then there is nothing left of Christianity but a philosophy.

By and large, and sadly so, the modern Church has eliminated the Cross from its thinking and from its preaching and teaching. Since the modern Church has changed the solution, it also must now change the problem; that's the reason it no longer refers to sin as sin.

But changing the definition does not change the problem, and ignoring the true solution does not supply another solution.

Let us say it again:

The problem of sin is so deadly, so powerful, so all-encompassing, so total, and so destructive that there is only one solution to this problem, and that is the Cross of Christ. *"The Law of Sin and Death"* yields to no other power except the Cross of Christ (Col. 2:14-15).

Chapter 3

The Law Of The Mind

CHAPTER THREE

THE LAW OF THE MIND

"But I see another Law in my members (the Law of Sin and Death desiring to use my physical body as an instrument of unrighteousness)*, warring against the Law of my Mind* (this is the Law of desire and will-power)*, and bringing me into captivity to the Law of sin* (the Law of Sin and Death) *which is in my members* (which will function through my members, and make me a slave to the Law of Sin and Death; this will happen to the most consecrated Christian if that Christian doesn't constantly exercise faith in Christ and the Cross, understanding that it is through the Cross that all powers of darkness were defeated [Col. 2:14-15])*"* (Rom. 7:23).

When any person comes to Christ, immediately their disposition changes. Before conversion, the sin nature ruled them in totality, but now they are dominated by the *"Divine Nature"* (II Pet. 1:4). As such, the Believer no longer desires to sin; he will struggle against sin with all of his might and power. In fact, the thought of sin is repugnant to him. He once loved transgression, but now it is most distasteful.

However, even though the new Believer is now a new creation in Christ Jesus, with old things having passed away, and all things becoming new, still if he doesn't function according to God's Prescribed Order — which is Faith placed exclusively in Christ and the Cross — he will find himself failing (II Cor. 5:17; Rom. 7:15).

THE MIND AND THE WILL

One might say that the *"will"* is the trigger of the *"mind."* The mind and the will are two different things, but they are so similar that they are almost indivisible.

It should be obvious that the *"will"* is very important because it triggers an individual's desire to live for God. The Scripture plainly says, *"And whosoever will, let him take the Water of Life freely"* (Rev. 22:17). But yet the *"will"* of the human being is protected by God in only one capacity; if the individual so desires, and no matter what the problem, the individual can accept Christ. This means that the drunkard or the drug addict, even though they are so bound by these viles that they cannot stop, can still say *"Yes"* to the Lord Jesus, if they so desire, and even though they do not have the capabilities to say *"No"* to alcohol or drugs. The Word of God means what it says, *"Whosoever will. . . ."*

After the person comes to Christ, the routine remains the same. The individual has the willpower to say *"Yes"* to Christ, but when he tries to use that willpower as a vehicle for overcoming sin, he will fare little better than his unsaved counterpart trying to say *"No"* to vices such as alcohol and drugs.

However, most Christians do not understand this. Most Christians might understand that before they were saved, they couldn't say *"No"* to certain things, but most also have the mistaken idea that now that they are saved, the Lord has given them a greater willpower, so they in turn can say *"No"* to sin.

This is false! They can't! They are looking at it in the wrong way, and that's not what the Bible teaches.

After a person comes to Christ, their willpower doesn't change. They are <u>not</u> given some type of super-willpower, as most think.

IS SIN A CHOICE?

In a sense, yes it is. However, it's not a choice in the way and manner that it is mostly taught.

Most teach that if a Christian sins, it is simply because they have made the choice to do so. In other words, all they had to do was simply say *"No"* to the sin and the problem would be solved. So, according to these false teachers, if a Christian yields to the sin, this shows that the person was not very sincere to begin with, and they attribute all manner of evil characteristics to him.

None of that is correct!

As we have previously stated, no true Christian wants to sin. If that Christian has taken an erroneous direction, his flesh may cry for some unlawful things, but sin is nevertheless repugnant to any true Christian. Actually, when a true Christian sins, he can't wait to ask the Lord to forgive him and for that thing to be washed by the Blood of Jesus (I Jn. 1:9).

So the idea that a Christian wants to sin and does so with impunity is totally incorrect!

So why do Christians sin?

Christians sin simply because they do not know God's Prescribed Order of Victory, which means that they are facing the situation in all the wrong ways. They are facing it with their willpower, and they may win a few rounds in this manner, but after a while they are going to lose.

Listen to Paul. The great Apostle said, and I quote from *THE EXPOSITOR'S STUDY BIBLE*:

"For I know that in me (that is, in my flesh,) dwells no good thing (speaks of man's own ability, or rather the lack thereof in comparison to the

Holy Spirit, at least when it comes to spiritual things): *for to will is present with me* (Paul is speaking here of his willpower; regrettably, most modern Christians are trying to live for God by means of willpower, thinking falsely that since they have come to Christ, they are now free to say *'No'* to sin; that is the wrong way to look at the situation; the Believer cannot live for God by the strength of willpower; while the will is definitely important, it alone is not enough; the Believer must exercise Faith in Christ and the Cross, and do so constantly; then he will have the ability and strength to say *'Yes'* to Christ, which automatically says *'No'* to the things of the world); *but how to perform that which is good I find not* (outside of the Cross, it is impossible to find a way to do good)*"* (Rom. 7:18).

Emphatically, and even dogmatically, the Apostle here tells us that it is impossible to do that which is good by the means of willpower, that is, to live for God as one should live for God!

THE CHOICE A CHRISTIAN MAKES

Whether a Christian realizes it or not (and most do <u>not</u>!), the choice he makes is the choice of trusting exclusively in Christ and what Christ did at the Cross or trusting in other things. That, and that alone, is the choice that one makes.

Sadly, most Christians do not understand the Cross and Sanctification (that is, how we are to live for God); as a result, most make the choice to go in directions other than the Cross. Even though this happens mostly through ignorance, the result is the same — failure!

THE STRUGGLE WITH SIN

If the Believer is struggling with sin, the Believer is fighting the wrong fight, at the wrong time, and at the wrong place. At the Cross of Calvary, Jesus Christ faced sin in all of its forms and took all of its penalty (the penalty was death!), and thereby atoned for all sin – past, present, and future — at least for all who will believe. In other words, Jesus has defeated sin in every capacity, because he has defeated the originator of sin, who is the Devil (Col. 2:14–15).

Our Lord not only defeated Satan at the Cross, and did so by atoning for all sin, which is the means by which Satan holds man in captivity, but Christ did so in such a way that the defeat of the Evil One is known throughout the entire spirit world. The Scripture says:

"And you, being dead in your sins and the uncircumcision of your flesh (speaks of spiritual death [that is, *'separation from God'*], which sin does!)*, has He quickened together with Him* (refers to being made

spiritually alive, which is done through being *'born again'*), *having forgiven you all trespasses* (the Cross made it possible for all manner of sin to be forgiven and taken away);

"Blotting out the handwriting of Ordinances that was against us (pertains to the Law of Moses, which was God's Standard of Righteousness that man could not reach), *which was contrary to us* (Law is against us, simply because we are unable to keep its precepts, no matter how hard we try), *and took it out of the way* (refers to the penalty of the Law being removed), *nailing it to His Cross* (the Law with its decrees was abolished in Christ's Death, as if crucified with Him);

"And having spoiled principalities and powers (Satan and all of his henchmen were defeated at the Cross by Christ atoning for all sin; sin was the legal right Satan had to hold man in captivity; with all sin atoned, he has no more legal right to hold anyone in bondage), *He* (Christ) *made a show of them openly* (what Jesus did at the Cross was in the face of the whole universe), *triumphing over them in it."* (The triumph is complete and it was all done for us, meaning we can walk in power and perpetual victory due to the Cross)*"* (Col. 2:13-15).

Although Satan will continue to tempt Believers through his agents, demon spirits, the Believer still can come to the place that there is no longer a struggle with sin. He understands that the struggle was faced, addressed, and handled some 2,000 years ago at Calvary's Cross. Jesus Christ has fought this battle and won this battle in totality.

If the Believer places his faith exclusively in Christ and what Christ did at the Cross, which is the choice the Believer must make, that is, if perpetual victory is to be obtained, then he will accrue to himself that for which Jesus paid such a price. This is what True Christianity actually is. This is what Jesus was talking about when He spoke of *"more abundant life"* (Jn. 10:10).

Far too many Believers are attempting to do what Christ has already done for us, which we cannot do for ourselves anyway. When a Believer takes such a path, that is, attempting to do what only Christ can do, this is a direct insult to Christ and what He did for us at the Cross. I am certain that the Lord is not too very much pleased with such conduct. Such action states to the whole world that what Jesus did was not enough and there has to be some things added to His great Work. But the Scripture plainly bears out that what He did at the Cross is a *"Finished Work"* (Jn. 19:30).

THE RENEWED MIND

Paul also stated: *"I beseech you therefore, Brethren,* (I beg of you please), *by the Mercies of God* (all is given to the Believer, not because of merit on the Believer's part, but strictly because of the *"Mercy of God"*), *that you present your bodies a Living Sacrifice* (the word *"Sacrifice"* speaks of the Sacrifice of Christ, and means that we cannot do this which the Holy Spirit demands unless our Faith is placed strictly in Christ and the Cross, which then gives the Holy Spirit latitude to carry out this great work within our lives), *holy* (that which the Holy Spirit Alone can do), *acceptable unto God* (actually means that a holy physical body, that is, *"temple,"* is all that He will accept), *which is your reasonable service* (reasonable if we look to Christ and the Cross; otherwise impossible!).

"And be not conformed to this world (the ways of the world)*: but be ye transformed by the renewing of your mind* (we must start thinking spiritually, which refers to the fact that everything is furnished to us through the Cross, and is obtained by Faith and not works), *that you may prove what is that good* (is put to the test and finds that the thing tested meets the specifications laid down) *and acceptable, and perfect, Will of God* (presents that which the Holy Spirit is attempting to bring about within our lives, and can only be obtained by ever making the Cross the Object of our Faith)*"* (Rom. 12:1-2).

The *"renewing of the mind"* begins the moment a person comes to Christ. It is not done overnight, and it's not done quickly. The mind of the newly-converted Believer has been accustomed to thinking totally in the realm of unbelief, of sin, and of ways which always are opposite of God. There actually is no way that the unconverted man or woman can think anything that is of God, that is, that it be acceptable to God.

So, when the person comes to Christ, the education then begins.

HOW IS THE MIND RENEWED?

It is renewed by the Holy Spirit through the Word of God. The Holy Spirit does nothing except it is totally and completely according to the Word of God.

The Holy Spirit does such by Revelation, and only by Revelation.

What does that mean?

It simply means that the Holy Spirit illuminates the Word to the Believer, gives him understanding and does so by various different means.

Again, Paul said, and I continue to quote from *THE EXPOSITOR'S STUDY BIBLE*:

"And He gave (our Lord does the calling) *some, Apostles* (has references to the fact that not all who are called to be Ministers will be called to be Apostles; this applies to the other designations as well; *'Apostles'* serve as the de facto leaders of the Church, and do so through the particular Message given to them by the Lord for the Church)*; and*

some, Prophets (who stand in the Office of the Prophet, thereby, fore-telling and forth-telling); *and some, Evangelists* (to gather the harvest); *and some, Pastors* (Shepherds) *and Teachers* (those with a special Ministry to teach the Word to the Body of Christ; 'Apostles' can and do function in all of the callings);

"For the perfecting of the Saints (to 'equip for service'), *for the work of the Ministry* (to proclaim the Message of Redemption to the entirety of the world), *for the edifying of the Body of Christ* (for the spiritual building up of the Church):

"Till we all come in the unity of the Faith (to bring all Believers to a proper knowledge of Christ and the Cross), *and of the knowledge of the Son of God* (which again refers to what He did for us at the Cross), *unto a perfect man* (the Believer who functions in maturity), *unto the measure of the stature of the fullness of Christ* (the 'measure' is the 'fullness of Christ,' which can only be attained by a proper Faith in the Cross):

"That we henceforth be no more children (presents the opposite of maturity, and speaks of those whose faith is in that other than the Cross), *tossed to and fro, and carried about with every wind of doctrine, by the sleight of men* (Satan uses Preachers), *and cunning craftiness* (they make a way, other than the Cross, which seems to be right), *whereby they lie in wait to deceive* (refers to a deliberate planning or system);

"But speaking the Truth in Love (powerfully proclaiming the Truth of the Cross, but always with Love), *may grow up into Him in all things* (proper Spiritual Growth can take place only according to proper Faith in the Cross [I Cor. 1:21, 23; 2:2]), *which is the Head, even Christ.* (Christ is the Head of the Church, and is such by virtue of the Cross)" (Eph. 4:11-15).

The Apostle also said, *"But as it is written* (Isa. 64:4), *Eye has not seen, nor ear heard, neither have entered into the heart of man* (the purpose is to show that we cannot come to a knowledge of God through these normal ways of learning), *the things which God has prepared for them who love Him."*

"But God has revealed them unto us by His Spirit (tells us the manner of impartation of Spiritual Knowledge, which is Revelation): *for the Spirit searches all things, yes, the deep things of God.* (The Holy Spirit is the only One amply qualified to reveal God because He is God, and He is the Member of the Godhead Who deals directly with man)" (I Cor. 2:9-10).

THE DEGREE OF MATURITY OF THE BELIEVER IS PREDICATED ON THE KNOWLEDGE OF THE CROSS

I want you to read that Heading again, inasmuch as it is very, very important.

The Cross of Christ in actuality is the story of the Bible. So if one is to properly know the Word of God, one also must properly know the Cross. The degree of one's maturity will depend on such knowledge.

Paul said, *"For Christ sent me not to baptize* (presents to us a Cardinal Truth), *but to preach the Gospel* (the manner in which one may be saved from sin)*: not with wisdom of words* (intellectualism is not the Gospel), *lest the Cross of Christ should be made of none effect.* (This tells us in no uncertain terms that the Cross of Christ must always be the emphasis of the Message)*"* (I Cor. 1:17).

In this one Verse, we are plainly and clearly told what the Gospel of Jesus Christ, which is the Gospel of the Word of God, actually is. It is *"The Cross of Christ."* In other words, if one is not preaching the Cross, is not looking to the Cross, is not looking exclusively to the Cross, then one is not embracing the Gospel of Jesus Christ.

The Believer must understand that Christ is the Source and the Cross is the Means.

Most Believers have no difficulty or problem with the idea of Christ as the Source. However, when it comes to the Cross as the Means, this is where the problem arises. To properly understand the Gospel, the Believer must understand that every single thing that we receive from the Lord (and I mean everything!) comes to us exclusively through Christ as the Source and the Cross as the Means. It is the Cross which has made everything possible.

Whatever the Lord is presently, He has always been. In other words, He doesn't have more power now than He had ten thousand years ago.

The question always has been, *"How could a thrice-Holy God deal with man, who is in such a sinful condition?"*

The only way He could is by and through the Cross of Christ. That's the reason it is imperative that all Believers make the Cross the only Object of their Faith. There is no other means than the Cross by which Jesus Christ purchased man's Redemption and made possible more abundant life. We must never forget that!

So, the *"mind"* of the individual, within itself, cannot effect Victory in one's life. The desire is there, and the will is there, but as Paul said, *"how to perform it"* (Rom. 7:18) is something else again. When the Lord gave to the Apostle the great Revelation of the Cross, he would learn that God's Way is the Way of the Cross. We say this over and over again. The Believer must, therefore, ever make the Cross of Christ the Object of his Faith (Rom. 6:1-14; 8:1-2, 11).

Chapter 4

The Law Of The Spirit Of Life In Christ Jesus

CHAPTER FOUR

THE LAW OF THE SPIRIT OF LIFE IN CHRIST JESUS

Paul said, *"There is therefore now no condemnation* (guilt) *to them which are in Christ Jesus* (refers back to Rom. 6:3-5 and our being Baptized into His Death, which speaks of the Crucifixion)*, who walk not after the flesh* (depending on one's personal strength and ability or great religious efforts in order to overcome sin)*, but after the Spirit* (the Holy Spirit works exclusively within the legal confines of the Finished Work of Christ; our Faith in that Finished Work, that is, *'the Cross,'* guarantees the help of the Holy Spirit, which guarantees Victory).

"For the Law (that which we are about to give is a Law of God, devised by the Godhead in eternity past [I Pet. 1:18-20]; this Law, in fact, is *'God's Prescribed Order of Victory') of the Spirit* (Holy Spirit, that is, *'the Way the Spirit works') of Life* (all life comes from Christ, but through the Holy Spirit [Jn. 16:13-14]) *in Christ Jesus* (any time Paul uses this term, or one of its derivatives, he is, without fail, referring to what Christ did at the Cross, which makes this *'life'* possible) *has made me free* (given me total Victory) *from the Law of Sin and Death.* (These are the two most powerful Laws in the Universe; the *'Law of the Spirit of Life in Christ Jesus'* alone is stronger than the *'Law of Sin and Death'*; this means that if the Believer attempts to live for God by any manner other than Faith in Christ and the Cross, he is doomed to failure)*"* (Rom. 8:1-2).

As we have said elsewhere in this Volume, the second most powerful Law in the world is *"The Law of Sin and Death."* But the most powerful Law, thank God, is *"The Law of the Spirit of Life in Christ Jesus."*

This most important Law is so very, very important; so, even though we explained it in the Text above, we will continue on and address it a little more fully.

Proper exegesis of the Scriptural Text shows us that *"The Law of the Spirit of Life in Christ Jesus"* is triggered by the Finished Work of Christ. When, as stated, the Apostle Paul uses the term *"in Christ Jesus,"* or any one of its many derivatives (such as *"in Him," "in Whom," "in Christ,"* etc.), without fail, he is speaking of the Cross and what Jesus did there. This refers to the way the Holy Spirit works, which means that He works entirely within the parameters of the Finished Work of Christ. In other words, it is the Cross which gives the Holy Spirit the legal right to do all the things which He does, all on behalf of Believers.

There is only one thing required for this *"Law"* to go into effect in our lives, to stay in effect, and to give us perpetual Victory, and that one thing is Faith.

FAITH

Paul said, *"Likewise reckon* (account) *you also yourselves to be dead indeed unto* (the) *sin* (while the sin nature is not dead, we are dead unto the sin nature by virtue of the Cross and our Faith in that Sacrifice, but only as long as our Faith continues in the Cross), *but alive unto God* (living the Resurrection Life) *through Jesus Christ our Lord* (refers to what He did at the Cross, which is the means of this Resurrection Life)*"* (Rom. 6:11).

In effect, the Holy Spirit through Paul is telling the Believer to reach back to Verses 3 through 5 of the Sixth Chapter of Romans, ever making that the Object of our Faith, which is the intention.

The word *"reckon"* in the Greek is *"logizomai,"* which means *"to take an inventory, to conclude, to impute, to number."*

Concerning Abraham, the Scripture says, *"And he believed in the LORD; and He counted it to him for Righteousness"* (Gen. 15:6).

The word *"counted,"* as used here, means the same thing as *"reckon."* It pertains to faith, and more particularly to what the object of faith must be.

Before the Cross, the Lord only asked that Believers do just that – believe in what was to come in the future, namely Christ (Gen. 3:15). In fact, the word *"faith"* is used only two times in the Old Testament (Deut. 32:20; Hab. 2:4).

The word *"believe"* was used in the place of the word *"faith,"* and both actually mean the same thing.

Even though the Cross of Christ was ever to be the Object of Faith, even from the very beginning, still, there was only a dim outline given of the coming Sacrifice and the way it would take place. It was to Abraham that the Lord proclaimed the fact that it would be by *"death"* that man would be redeemed. It was at the proposed offering of Isaac. The Scripture says, *"And Abraham called the name of that place Jehovah-Jireh,"* which means *"The LORD will provide."*

Provide what?

Provide a Redeemer, Who would be the Lord Jesus Christ.

However, even though the Lord proclaimed to Abraham that it would be by death that man would be redeemed, still He did not tell the Patriarch exactly how or what that death would be. That remained unto the time of Moses.

Israel had sinned greatly, *"And the LORD sent fiery serpents among the people, and they bit the people; and much people of Israel died"* (Num. 21:6).

The people came to Moses, and Moses went to the Lord. The Lord told him, *"Make thee a fiery serpent, and set it upon a pole: and it shall come to pass, that everyone who is bitten, when he looks upon it, shall live"* (Num. 21:8).

Jesus alluded to this in his conversation with Nicodemus (Jn. 3:14-21).

The Lord told Abraham *"how"* Redemption would come, which would be by death, but He told Moses what *"manner of death"* it would be. It would be the Cross. There Jesus paid the debt for all sin — past, present, and future — at least for all who will believe (Jn. 3:16).

THE LAW

As we have previously stated, Romans 8:2 presents a *"Law."* Furthermore, this is a Law that was devised by the Godhead sometime in eternity past (I Pet. 1:18-20). The use by the Holy Spirit of the term *"Law"* tells us that the Lord will not deviate from this Word. He said exactly what He meant, and meant exactly what He said.

If we function according to this *"Law of the Spirit of Life in Christ Jesus,"* we will reap the benefits which this Law promises. It promises us victory over *"the Law of Sin and Death."* The only way we can have victory over *"the Law of Sin and Death"* is by putting into practice into our lives the only Law in the Universe which is stronger, namely, *"The Law of the Spirit of Life in Christ Jesus."*

We do all this strictly by faith. We simply believe and reckon ourselves that we have died with Him, we were buried with Him by baptism into death, and were raised with Him in newness of life (Rom. 6:3-5). If we live by this Law, function by this Law, abide by this Law, and allow it to be the guiding force in our lives, which can be summed up totally and completely in the Cross of Christ, we will accrue to ourselves the results which this Law guarantees, which is total and complete victory over the Law of Sin and Death.

That is the Lord's answer to sin! His answer to iniquity! His answer to transgression! His answer to all failure!

This is the reason the Church is so foolish as to resort to humanistic psychology. It becomes even worse when we realize that humanistic psychology holds no help whatsoever. It is a broken cistern that can hold no water. The answer is in the Cross of Christ; and the answer is only in the Cross of Christ, which given the Holy Spirit latitude to work in our lives, without which we cannot properly live this Christian experience.

THE HOLY SPIRIT

While Christ is the Source, and the Cross is the Means, it is the Holy

Spirit Who makes available to the Believer all that Christ has paid for at the Cross. In fact, anything and everything that is done within our lives respecting the Lord, is carried out exclusively by and through the Ministry, Office, and Person of the Holy Spirit. In fact, every single thing that's been done on this Earth in the realm of the Godhead, other than what Christ did at Calvary's Cross, has been done by and through the Holy Spirit. To clarify the point, one might say that God the Father is the Owner, God the Son is the Architect, and God the Holy Spirit is the Builder. And of course, all three Persons of the Godhead function in every capacity, as should be obvious, but at the same time, it is the Holy Spirit Who actually does the Work of God on Earth (Gen. 1:1-2). In fact, the Bible begins by the Holy Spirit *"moving,"* and closes with the Holy Spirit saying *"come"* to a lost and dying world (Rev. 22:17). So, whatever is done within our hearts and lives, whether it be Fruit of the Spirit, or Gifts of the Spirit, or Spiritual Growth of any nature, which includes bearing fruit for the Lord, all and without question are carried out through the Office, the Ministry, and Person of the Holy Spirit. One of the great sins of the modern Church is trying to take the place of the Holy Spirit, and doing so by introducing various schemes and programs, etc.

HOW DOES THE HOLY SPIRIT WORK?

Regrettably, the greater majority of the modern Church little knows or understands as to how the Holy Spirit functions and operates within our lives. Most simply take Him for granted, that is if they think about Him at all.

The Holy Spirit works within our hearts and lives strictly through and by the Finished Work of Christ, in other words, what Christ did for us at the Cross. That is what gives Him the legal right to carry out His Work (Rom. 8:2).

As we've already stated in this Volume, even several times, He doesn't demand much of us, but He does demand Faith. More particularly, He demands that our Faith ever be in the Cross of Christ as its Object (Rom. 6:1-14). When our faith is properly placed, and our faith remains in the Cross, then the Holy Spirit can carry out His Work within our hearts and lives, which He Alone can do.

Unfortunately, the far greater majority of the modern Church has everything in the world as the object of its faith other than the Cross of Christ. While the Holy Spirit does not leave such an individual, continuing to do all that He can do, still, He is greatly hindered by our improper faith (Rom. 8:11).

FAILING CHRISTIANS!

In fact, at this very moment, there are millions of Christians who truly love the Lord, and are trying to do their very best to serve Him with all of their heart; however, despite all of their efforts they are failing and the simple truth is, they don't know why. Paul addressed this by saying:

"For that which I do (the failure) *I allow not* (should have been translated, *'I understand not'*; these are not the words of an unsaved man, as some claim, but rather a Believer who is trying and failing)*: for what I would, that do I not* (refers to the obedience he wants to render to Christ, but rather fails; why? As Paul explained, the Believer is married to Christ, but is being unfaithful to Christ by spiritually cohabiting with the Law, which frustrates the Grace of God; that means the Holy Spirit will not help such a person, which guarantees failure [Gal. 2:21]*; but what I hate, that do I* (refers to sin in his life which he doesn't want to do, and in fact hates, but finds himself unable to stop; unfortunately, due to the fact of not understanding the Cross as it refers to Sanctification, this is the plight of most modern Christians)*"* (Rom. 7:15).

As we stated in the notes, the phrase *"I allow not,"* should have been translated *"I understand not,"* because that's what it actually means.

Millions of modern Christians are struggling with all of their strength and might and failing just the same, which places them in a position of not understanding what is happening.

They know they love the Lord! They know that they are Born-Again! Many of them are even baptized with the Holy Spirit, and many of them are even being used by God in some way, but yet in their own personal life they are failing. Unfortunately, these are not isolated cases, but rather, sadly, the norm.

It is because their faith is placed in something other than the Cross of Christ, which means they have hindered the Work of the Holy Spirit within their lives, which always guarantees failure, and no matter how hard they try otherwise.

Incidentally, when Paul wrote this in the Seventh Chapter of Romans, he most definitely knew and understood at that time the means of God's victorious living, which is the Cross of Christ; however, he struggled for several years before this great Revelation was given to him, hence, him writing this Seventh Chapter of Romans relating to us his experience. And please let the reader understand, if Paul could not successfully live for God without an understanding of the Cross and faith thereby properly applied, how do we think we can do so?

As stated, the Holy Spirit works entirely within the parameters of the great Finished Work of Christ, i.e., *"the Atonement."* That is where we must place our faith.

I would advise the reader to secure for yourself our study guide *THE CROSS OF CHRIST, How The Holy Spirit Works.*

Chapter 5

The Law Of Faith

CHAPTER FIVE

THE LAW OF FAITH

I'm sure the Reader has noticed by now that we quote the Apostle Paul quite frequently. We do this not at all to take away from the other Bible writers, but rather because it was to Paul that the meaning of the New Covenant, that is, *"the Cross,"* was given (Gal. 1:11-12). In fact, everything that Simon Peter, as well as John the Beloved and every other Apostle of that particular time, learned about the Cross came from the teaching of the Apostle Paul. The Holy Spirit meant in no way to demean these other great Apostles. He simply chose the Apostle Paul to be the one to whom He gave this great Revelation.

We aren't told why the Holy Spirit chose Paul. But this we do know:

The world owes a debt of gratitude that it never can repay to the Jew from Tarsus. What we today refer to as *"Western Civilization"* is due mostly to the Apostle Paul. But yet, he was only the bearer of the Message; the Crown Prince was, and is, the Lord Jesus Christ.

The great Apostle said, *"To declare, I say, at this time His Righteousness* (refers to God's Righteousness, which must be satisfied at all times, and is in Christ and only Christ)*: that He* (God) *might be just* (not overlooking sin in any manner), *and the justifier of him which believes in Jesus* (God can justify a believing [although guilty] sinner and His Holiness not be impacted, providing the sinner's Faith is exclusively in Christ; only in this manner can God be *'just'* and at the same time *'Justify'* the sinner).

"Where is boasting then? (This refers primarily to the Jews boasting of themselves as a result of the Law of God given to them, but the principle is true for modern Christians as well!) *It is excluded* (not only means that God will not accept such boasting [outside of Christ], but that it actually serves to keep one from Salvation). *By what Law? Of works?* (In a sense, this tells us where and how the boasting, God will not accept, originates.) *No: but by the Law of Faith* (refers to trust exclusively in Christ and what He did at the Cross; faith in Christ and Him crucified is more than a principle; it is a Law, meaning that God will not deviate at all from this proclamation)*"* (Rom. 3:26-27).

WHAT IS THE LAW OF FAITH?

It is the simple fact that God will pardon a sinner and forgive a Believer simply on the basis of that individual exhibiting Faith in Christ and what Christ did for us at the Cross.

53

God's Justification of a sinner is an action of His Grace based upon, and because of, the Redemption that is in Christ Jesus. It is only because of Christ's atoning Sacrifice that God will not only pardon but justify sinners (Rom. 3:24-25).

All sins committed by the people of God prior to, and up to, the one great Sacrifice of Calvary were put upon one side by God in His forbearance, which, in effect, was awaiting Calvary, and then judged there; and all sins committed since Calvary were equally judged there. Thus, the Cross of Calvary stands at the center of human history.

As we have repeatedly stated: Everything hinges on the Cross. It was there that Jesus paid the price, and paid it fully. It was there that all sins were atoned, past, present, and future. It was there that all Salvation was effected. It was there that all victory was won. It was there that Satan was totally and completely defeated, along with all of his minions of darkness!

If the believing sinner is to be saved, and if the Christian is to have perpetual victory within his life, it is a *"Law"* that the individual must express Faith in Christ and what Christ did for us at the Cross for such to be.

Once again, whenever the word *"Law"* is used, it means that God will not deviate from this manner and way. He will not save sinners on the basis of merit or works. Likewise, He will not give Christians victory on the basis of merit or works! He will function only on the basis of Faith, and more particularly the correct Object of Faith, which is *"Jesus Christ and Him Crucified."*

Anytime Paul speaks of faith, he is speaking of the Cross of Christ as the correct Object of Faith (I Cor. 1:17-18, 23; 2:2; Gal. 2:20-21; Chpt. 5; 6:14).

THE CORRECT OBJECT OF FAITH

There probably have been more books written on faith in the last fifty years than in all the balance of Christendom put together. But yet the modern Church probably is evidencing less faith at present (and we speak of true Faith) than at any time since the Reformation. In fact, the modern Church is almost faithless.

How do I know that?

The reason is that the correct object of faith is not known.

If Believers are asked what they mean by the word *"faith"* or how they are to exercise faith, most probably would answer that they are to believe God's Word. That certainly is true. However, most of the time, that which says too much really says nothing.

Most Christians do not understand what the correct object of their faith ought to be. Neither do they understand that if the object of faith is wrong, then their faith doesn't amount to much.

The truth is, every human being in this world has faith. It is not faith in God, but it is nevertheless faith. We ride in automobiles because Henry Ford knew how to establish an assembly line. We fly in airplanes because of the Wright Brothers. Bill Gates became the richest man in the world because he had faith in his ability to write programs for computer systems.

But the faith evidenced by these individuals was not the faith that God would recognize. Furthermore, most Christians evidence faith that God little recognizes.

Let us say this bluntly, plainly, and clearly:

THE ONLY FAITH THAT GOD WILL RECOGNIZE IS THAT WHICH HAS THE CROSS AS ITS OBJECT

Because it is so very, very important, let us say that again.

The only faith that God will recognize (that is, faith that God will act upon) is Faith which has as its Object the Cross of Christ. Listen to what Jesus said about this:

"And He said to them all, If any man will come after Me (the criteria for Discipleship), *let him deny himself* (not asceticism as many think, but rather that one denies one's own willpower, self-will, strength, and ability, depending totally on Christ), *and take up his cross* (the benefits of the Cross, looking exclusively to what Jesus did there to meet our every need) *daily* (this is so important, our looking to the Cross, that we must renew our Faith in what Christ has done for us, even on a daily basis, for Satan will ever try to move us away from the Cross as the Object of our Faith, which always spells disaster), *and follow Me.* (Christ can be followed only by the Believer looking to the Cross, understanding what it accomplished, and by that means alone [Eph. 2:13-18; Col. 2:14-15])*"* (Lk. 9:23).

Listen again to what our Lord said. This statement is even more severe:

"And whosoever does not bear his Cross (this doesn't speak of suffering, as most think, but rather ever making the Cross of Christ the Object of our Faith; we are saved and we are victorious, not by suffering, although that sometimes will happen, or any other similar things, but rather by our Faith, but always with the Cross of Christ as the Object of that Faith), *and come after Me* (one can follow Christ only by Faith in what He has done for us at the Cross; He recognizes nothing else), *cannot be My Disciple.* (The statement is emphatic! If it's not Faith in the Cross of Christ, then it's faith that God will not recognize, which means that such people are refused [I Cor. 1:17-18, 21, 23; 2:2; Rom. 6:1-14; 8:1-2, 11, 13; Gal., Chpt. 5])*"* (Lk. 14:27).

So here, in no uncertain terms, the Lord tells us that if we do not take up our Cross and follow Him, then we cannot be His Disciple. Those are frightening words!

When one considers that virtually the entire modern Church has abandoned the Cross, then these statements by our Lord become even more frightening.

When our Lord says that something is a *"Law,"* He means exactly what He says. This means that if we want to have results, we cannot deviate from that Law; I speak, of course, of the positive Laws.

The Cross of Calvary, and what Jesus there did, is to be the Object of our Faith. That is a *"Law."* As stated, we must not deviate from this direction, this *"Law of Faith."*

Chapter 6

The Law Of Christ

CHAPTER SIX

THE LAW OF CHRIST

"Brethren, if a man be overtaken in a fault (pertains to moral failure, and is brought about because one has ignorantly placed himself under Law; such a position guarantees failure), *you which are Spiritual* (refers to those who understand God's Prescribed Order of Victory, which is the Cross), *restore such an one* (tell him he failed because of reverting to Law, and that victory can be his by placing his faith totally in the Cross, which then gives the Holy Spirit latitude to work, Who Alone can give the Victory) *in the spirit of meekness* (never with an overbearing, holier-than-thou attitude); *considering yourself, lest you also be tempted* (the implication is that if we do not handle such a case Scripturally, we thereby open the door for Satan to attack us in the same manner as he did the failing brother).

"Bear ye one another's burdens (refers to sharing the heartache and shame of one who has spiritually failed), *and so fulfill the Law of Christ* (which is Love!)*"* (Gal. 6:1-2).

WHAT IS THE LAW OF CHRIST?

The *"Law of Christ,"* as just stated, is *"Love."*

Perhaps in the case of a failing brother or sister, this particular *"Law"* is needed more than any other manner.

Why?

The world is very slow to forgive, and the Church forgives not at all! That is a tragedy, but oh so true!

In no way do these statements imply that we should condone sin, because sin cannot be condoned in any fashion. But when we deal with a brother or a sister who has sinned, our best course of action is to hear the words of James, *"There is one Lawgiver, Who is able to save and to destroy* (presents God as the only One Who can fill this position): *who are you who judges another?* (The Greek actually says, *'But you — who are you?'* In other words, *'who do you think you are?'*)*"* (James 4:12).

Paul also tells us to deal with such people with the *"spirit of meekness."*

AMONG CHRISTIANS, THERE
ARE TWO TYPES OF SINNERS

What do we mean by that Heading?

1. Some Christians actually have lost their way (which does not come

quickly or easily), and they now try to make allowances for their sin, which means they have no desire to quit what they are doing, but they try to have the Lord and sin at the same time. If such individuals continue on that path, they ultimately will lose their way altogether. Of such, the Lord said, *"I will spue* (vomit) *you out of My Mouth"* (Rev. 3:16).

Such words tell us that here there is no prospect of repentance or restoration. In fact, there is Divine rejection. Unless such a person comes to their spiritual senses, they will die eternally lost.

It is Faith in Christ and the Cross which gets the believing sinner into Salvation, and Faith in Christ and the Cross which keeps the person in Christ. Sin most definitely will erode that faith; if a person loses their faith, then the person loses their way completely, even as millions down through the many centuries have done.

In the first two Verses of the Sixth Chapter of Galatians, Paul addresses the second type of Christian who sins. This is the person who doesn't want to sin, who is trying not to sin, and who is struggling not to sin, but failing anyway.

Why is he failing?

He is failing simply because his faith is in something other than Christ and the Cross. The object of his faith may be something good in its own right, but if it's not the Cross of Christ, the Holy Spirit will little help such a person. The Spirit will not help because He cannot do so, which will ensure failure on the part of that individual. Millions of Christians fall into this category. They neither know nor understand God's Prescribed Order of Victory, so they try to bring about victory by their own efforts and abilities.

The Lord labels such efforts *"flesh"*; regarding this, the Scripture plainly says, *"They who are in the flesh cannot please God"* (Rom. 8:8).

2. This second type of Christian is totally different than the first type of Christian described a few paragraphs back. This type of Christian wants to please God, wants to live right, wants to do the thing that is right, but finds himself (or herself) unable to do so, no matter how hard he (she) tries. His faith is in the wrong object, and until his faith is placed exclusively in Christ and the Cross, failure is going to be the ongoing result of their efforts. Nothing he does can stop the failure. Victory is found only in the Cross, and that goes for all Believers, no matter who they are.

CAN SATAN OVERRIDE A BELIEVER'S WILL?

We have already touched on this very important subject elsewhere in this Volume. But due to its very great significance, let's go a little deeper into our explanation.

Yes! Satan most definitely can override a Believer's will and force that

Believer to do something he doesn't want to do, something he is trying, with all his strength, not to do. This is not an isolated case, but rather something that happens each and every day, even millions of times. It is sad, but true!

But even though Satan is forcing the person against his will, this doesn't mean the person is not responsible for what they do. If any Believer fails the Lord, that person is responsible, is guilty, has sinned, and must ask the Lord to forgive and to cleanse (I Jn. 1:9).

God judges the person as guilty, despite the fact the person did not want to do what he did and actually fought against it. The reason is because that person chose a way of supposed victory other than God's Prescribed Order. In taking that position, the person has guaranteed failure for himself.

Listen again to Paul, and I continue to quote from *THE EXPOSITOR'S STUDY BIBLE*:

"For the good that I would I do not (if I depend on self, and not the Cross)*: but the evil which I would not* (don't want to do)*, that I do* (which is exactly what every Believer will do no matter how hard he tries to do otherwise, if he tries to live this life outside of the Cross [Gal. 2:20-21])*"* (Rom. 7:19).

Pure and simple, the Apostle Paul here tells us that he is trying with all of his strength to *"do good,"* that is, live right; but he finds that, despite all his efforts, he simply cannot do what he wants to do.

Then Paul tells us that he finds himself doing the evil which he doesn't want to do, despite all his efforts to keep from doing this. This proves exactly what I have been saying.

Many claim that these Verses refer to Paul's experience before his Salvation. However, there is no way the Seventh Chapter of Romans describes a *"before-conversion experience"* of Paul. No! This pertained to Paul after he was saved, after he was baptized with the Holy Spirit, after he was called to be an Apostle, but before he was given the Revelation of the Cross. In this Chapter, he is telling us that if we do not know and understand the Sixth Chapter of Romans, which tells us how to have victory over the sin nature and to walk in perpetual victory, then we are going to repeat the Seventh Chapter of Romans all over again. Tragically, that's the state of most Christians.

Even though most will not admit it, because they do not understand the Cross of Christ as it refers to Sanctification, most good Christians fall into the category of Paul's statement, *"O wretched man that I am! Who shall deliver me from the body of this death?"*

Let me quote it from *THE EXPOSITOR'S STUDY BIBLE*:

"O wretched man that I am! (Any Believer who attempts to live for

God outside of God's Prescribed Order, which is *'Jesus Christ and Him Crucified,'* will in fact live a wretched and miserable existence. This life can only be lived in one way, and that way is the Cross.) *Who shall deliver me from the body of this death?* (The minute he cries *'Who?'* he finds the path to Victory, for he is now calling upon a Person for help, and that Person is Christ; actually, the Greek Text is masculine, indicating a Person)*" (Rom. 7:24).

Such a Christian, no matter how hard he tries, is not going to be able to live a victorious life. He might live a victorious life for a while, but ultimately he will fail. To be victorious, to be an overcomer, to live as the Lord desires that we live, to live as we certainly ought to live, one must exercise their Faith constantly in Christ and the Cross, and not allow their Faith to be moved elsewhere at any cost. The Holy Spirit, Who works entirely within the Finished Work of Christ, will then help such a Believer and then *"sin will no longer dominate them"* (Rom. 6:14).

The reason?

The reason is that we no longer are under Law, but under Grace (Rom. 6:14). Any life that the Believer attempts to live outside of Faith in Christ and the Cross constitutes Law, and it will guarantee failure.

As I have been attempting to describe, when such a Christian fails, they don't need someone to condemn him or her. They need the love of Christ shown to them, that is, *"The Law of Love."* They need to be told why they failed, and how they can get on the right road, which is the road of the Cross (Lk. 9:23-24).

Chapter 7

The Law Of Liberty

CHAPTER SEVEN

THE LAW OF LIBERTY

James said, *"But whoso looks into the perfect Law of Liberty* (defines the whole body of revealed truth concerning the Word of God), *and continues therein* (there must be a continuous abiding in the Word), *he being not a forgetful hearer, but a doer of the work, this man shall be blessed in his deed* (obeying the Word of God brings great Blessing; however, the only way it can be obeyed is for the Believer to unequivocally place his faith in Christ and the Cross)*"* (James 1:25).

WHAT IS THE LAW OF LIBERTY?

It is the liberty to do the Will of God in the freedom in which the New Nature delights.

It is believed that the Epistle written by James is one of the earliest written, possibly written in the mid- or high-40's A.D. If so, it was written shortly before the great Revelation of the Cross was given to the Apostle Paul, or at least shortly thereafter. At any rate, James would have had little or no knowledge at all regarding the Cross of Christ and how it pertains to Salvation and victorious living.

But yet, his statement concerning *"the perfect Law of Liberty"* very adequately describes the overcoming life. Of course, it is the Holy Spirit Who gave James this phrase.

Probably about ten years after James wrote his Epistle, the Apostle Paul wrote, *"Stand fast therefore in the Liberty wherewith Christ has made us free* (we were made free, and refers to freedom to live a Holy life by evidencing Faith in Christ and the Cross), *and be not entangled again with the yoke of bondage* (to abandon the Cross and go under Law of any kind guarantees bondage once again to the sin nature)*"* (Gal. 5:1).

HOW DOES LAW GUARANTEE
BONDAGE TO THE SIN NATURE?

While the Law of God, that is, the Law of Moses, is God's Standard of Righteousness and is, therefore, holy and pure, still, due to the Fall, man, even believing man, simply cannot keep its precepts, at least if he tries to do so by his own power and ability.

Since man lacks ability, God would become Man in order to do for man what man could not do for himself, which was to keep the Law perfectly, which Christ did, and then to go to the Cross in order to satisfy the demands of the broken Law. Jesus did all of that for us, simply because we could not do it for ourselves.

So, it is an insult to Christ for believing man to attempt to live for God by means of Law. Basically it calls God a liar. God says we cannot live it within ourselves and, therefore, He provided a Redeemer. When we try to live under Law, we are telling the Lord that we *can* live it by means of the Law, despite what He has said. In other words, we can keep the Law. But the truth is, we can't.

When the Believer turns from Law, and turns totally and completely to Christ and what Christ did at the Cross, then the Holy Spirit will help such a Believer, guaranteeing victory in every capacity (Rom. 8:1-2, 11). To make anything other than the Cross of Christ the object of one's faith constitutes spiritual adultery, which the Holy Spirit cannot condone. So if the Believer wants to try to live for God by means of Law, he never will be able to have *"The Law of Liberty"* functioning in his life, because the Holy Spirit will not help him in such an endeavor.

The moment the Believer places his faith exclusively in Christ and the Cross, understanding that everything we receive from God comes completely from Christ as the Source and the Cross as the Means, then the Holy Spirit, Who is God, and Who can do anything, will then begin to evidence His Might and Power on our behalf, which guarantees victory.

Please note the following simple formula:
1. FOCUS: The Lord Jesus Christ (Jn. 14:6).
2. OBJECT OF FAITH: The Cross of Christ (Rom. 6:1-14; Gal. 2:20-21).
3. POWER SOURCE: The Holy Spirit (Rom. 8:1-2, 11).
4. RESULTS: Victory (Rom. 6:14).

If the Reader will carefully study the little formula given above, I think it will explain satisfactorily that which we refer to as *"The Law of Liberty."* However, let's use the same formula, but let's address it in a different way.
1. FOCUS: Works.
2. OBJECT OF FAITH: Performance.
3. POWER SOURCE: Self.
4. RESULTS: Defeat.

THE EFFECT OF CHRIST

Paul said, *"Christ is become of no effect unto you* (this is a chilling statement, and refers to anyone who makes anything other than Christ and the Cross the Object of his Faith), *whosoever of you are Justified by the Law* (seek to be Justified by the Law)*; you are fallen from Grace* (fallen from the position of Grace, which means the Believer is trusting in something other than the Cross; it actually means *'to apostatize')"* (Gal. 5:4).

The Believer has a choice: he can function in *"The Law of the Spirit of Life in Christ Jesus"* or he will function in *"The Law of Sin and Death."* There is no other alternative.

"The Law of the Spirit of Life in Christ Jesus" can be summed up in the words, *"The Cross!" "The Cross!" "The Cross!"*

> *"Alas! And did my Saviour bleed?*
> *"And did my Sov'reign die?*
> *"Would He devote that sacred Head,*
> *"For such a worm as I?"*
>
> *"Was it for crimes that I had done,*
> *"He groaned upon the tree?*
> *"Amazing pity! Grace unknown!*
> *"And love beyond degree!"*
>
> *"Well might the sun in darkness hide,*
> *"And shut His glories in,*
> *"When Christ, the mighty Maker, died*
> *"For man the creature's sin."*
>
> *"Thus might I hide my blushing face,*
> *"While His dear Cross appears;*
> *"Dissolved my heart in thankfulness,*
> *"And melt my eyes to tears."*
>
> *"But drops of grief can ne'er repay*
> *"The debt of love I owe;*
> *"Here, Lord, I give myself away,*
> *"Tis all that I can do!"*

CHORUS:

> *"At the Cross, at the Cross, where I first saw the Light,*
> *"And the burden of my heart rolled away.*
> *"It was there by faith I received my sight,*
> *"And now I am happy all the day."*

**SELF-HELP
STUDY NOTES**